HOOKED

Funny Quotes
from
Serious Anglers

Published by:

Kitty Creek Press, Inc.
P.O. Box 5222
Austin, TX 78763
(512) 502-9670

ISBN 0-9627071-1-2

Printed on Recycled Paper.

Preface

I think of this book as a gift. A gift from the authors who created the original works and from the sport that has given me so much joy. It is a gift from me as an editor to you, the reader, and one which I hope you will share with someone else who loves to fish.

An after-dinner conversation with Mel Krieger, Sam Moore and Jim Ostrenga in front of the big stone fireplace at 4UR, a Colorado fly fishing resort, inspired this collection. We were there to help Mel conduct a fly-casting clinic and had spent the day on the lawn and on the Rio Grande River aiding Mel's students in their own quest for the "essence" of fly-casting.

A few of the students joined us for the inevitable recounting of the days' fishing experiences, and at some point our talk turned to fishing literature – to writers who fish and fishers who write, and who reads all those fishing stories anyway.

As we talked that evening, Mel mentioned Jim Harrison as an author whose work he admired. I wasn't familiar with the name and made some comment about how Harrison was probably just another macho guy swaggering around, talking big about his toys. Mel insisted Harrison was different, that he had something to say, that he said it well, and that he also possessed a sense of humor. We talked about other writers, but I only remember Harrison because Mel loaned me a copy of Harrison's collection of articles and essays, *Just Before Dark*. I read it, and I was hooked.

I returned to Austin and went directly to the bookstore. Today, in addition to my own copy of *Just Before Dark*, nine dog-eared and probably tear-stained volumes of Jim Harrison's work are clustered on my bookshelves. It's true. Sometimes Jim Harrison does swagger and talk big. I don't even care. I forgive him because he makes me laugh, and he makes me cry, and his observations about fishing are not confined to numbering dead fish. (Like many of the authors quoted in this book Harrison is not exclusively, or even especially, an angling writer, but images reflecting his love for angling abound in his work.) He communicates a sensitivity to life, to other living beings, and to the myriad frailties which pester all of us. He writes to us about his journey.

Intrigued by Harrison, I decided to explore the world of angling literature. Armed with Arnold Gingrich's charming exploration of the history of fly fishing literature, *Fishing in Print*, and later Verlyn Klinkenborg's suggested reading list (*Esquire Sportsman*, 1992) I headed for the libraries and bookstores. Like a ring in the water the ripple from the initial pebble that was Harrison widened. Each book led to several more.

I was in the middle of a hatch! I imagined fluttering caddislike open books emerging, multiplying and resting on every available surface. I could almost hear the whispery flapping of their black and white pages. Notebooks began to fill with lines I wanted to remember and share, and the plan for a book of quotations began to take shape.

I'm not going to lie and say my casting through the stream of fishing literature always netted writing as compelling or erudite as books by Toni Morrison or Dostoyevsky. To borrow Gingrich's phrase, some of it will "bore you blind." But there is much that is exceptional – funny, compelling, insightful, tender – and the writers share an abiding concern for the condition of humankind and the condition of our planet.

This small volume of very subjectively selected quotations is limited to some of the lines that made me smile. I hope these flashy attractors will cause you to scurry to your nearest library or bookstore to savor the complete, original work. To make that easy for you the source index in the back of this book is keyed to the page number where the quotation appears.

Meantime, the circle in the water widens, and the hatch is still on. If you've read something you'd like to share, I'm as near as your mailbox.

Raye Carrington
P.O. Box 5222
Austin, TX 78763

In Memoriam

Another one for Reba, my friend and mentor
in angling as well as other life lessons.

And for my dad,
R.B. "Mutt" Sheppard
(1911-1993)

Acknowledgements

I am way over the limit in debt to the effervescent and efficient Joene Grissom. She and her cadre of creative, talented professionals, Carlos Femat, Lee Lambert, and Mark Nathan leavened their serious attention to the design and production of this book with copious amounts of patience, good humor, and encouragement.

My life is nurtured by enthusiastic, smart, energetic, generous, loving friends and family, and everybody had suggestions! I especially want to thank two of my favorite fishing partners, Sam Sheppard and Houston Carrington; those two tireless trekkers and fishers, Joan Baker and Marcia Bailey and their spouses, Richard and Bob; my son, Charles Carrington and his wife Rolinda; the Austin Angler's Larry Sunderland; Mel Krieger, Cindy Garner, Bea Ann Smith, Velma Jordan, Edith Brown, Molly Lamphear, Sandy Silver; my Stitch and Bitch buddies, Immie, LaVada, Jackie, Judy, Janet, Mary, Bobbie, Andrea, and Selinda; and finally, my beautiful mother, Celia Sheppard, whose boundless love and wisdom I still find amazing.

Our tradition
[of the modern fisherman]
is that of the first man
who sneaked away to the creek
when the tribe
did not really need fish....

Roderick Haig-Brown

Fishermen
are born honest,
but they get over it.

Ed Zern

A fishing rod is a stick
with a hook at one end
and a fool at the other.

attributed to
Samuel Johnson

The more you fish
the more you start seeing these things
the way a farmer does:
it doesn't have to be great,
just please don't let it be awful.

John Gierach

[F]ishing
seems to me to be divided,
like sex,
into three most unequal parts,
the two larger of which, by far,
are anticipation and recollection,
and in between,
by far the smallest of the three,
actual performance.

Arnold Gingrich

Some men
would rather be
photographed with their fish
than with their wives....

Gwen Cooper
and Evelyn Haas

There are
so many permutations
of flies available
that choosing one sends most
people back to the decision,
"Do I use the entire worm or
do I cut it in two?"

Jack Ohman

On lightweight rods:

My friend Orvis Fenwick
once made half a dozen casts
before he realized
he hadn't picked up his rod.

Patrick F. McManus

8

Here lies Tommy Montague,
Whose love for Angling Daily grew;
He died regretted, while late out,
To make a capture of a trout.

Robert Blakey
(1856)

On average,
trout fishermen
will walk about as far
from the parking lot
as sunbathers.

M.R. Montgomery

Fishing tournaments
seem a little like playing tennis
with living balls,
say, neatly bound bluebirds.

Jim Harrison

If I didn't have
male fishing buddies,
I wouldn't have many
fishing buddies at all.

Mary S. Kuss

"You know why
there are so many whitefish
in the Yellowstone River?
Because the Fish and Game people
have never done anything
to help them."

Russell Chatham

There ain't but one time
to go fishin'
and that's
whenever you can.

Diron Talbert

The Gods do not deduct
from man's allotted span
the hours spent in fishing.

Babylonian Proverb
(often quoted by
Herbert Hoover)

Women fishermen:
Avoid them....
Avoid all of them
like woodticks.

Robert Traver

We ask a simple question
And that is all we wish:
Are fishermen all liars?
Or do only liars fish?

William Sherwood Fox

Creeps and idiots
cannot conceal themselves for long
on a fishing trip.

John Gierach

When you find someone
who answers all the questions,
you can be sure
that he doesn't fish enough
to know what it's all about,
or else-
well, just or else.

Ray Bergman

Trout are not looking
for something new and different,
to eat or do.

Arnold Gingrich

[A] trout
that doesn't think
two jumps
and several runs ahead
of the average fisherman
is mighty apt
to get fried.

Beatrice Cook

That one does not fish for trout
[in England]
with spinning lures or with live bait
is taken for granted,
along with toilet training.

William Humphrey

[R]egardless
of what you may think
of our penal system,
the fact is
that every man in jail
is one less potential fisherman
to clutter up your favorite pool or pond.

Ed Zern

If fishing
interferes with your
business,
give up your
business.

Sparse Grey Hackle

All fishermen
have the big-fish complex–
we want one bigger
than we have caught before,
something just a little bigger
than it's reasonable to hope for...

Roderick Haig-Brown

[I]f all the reasons for going a-fishing
that mankind has ever put forth
were packed into a great compendium
they would simmer down
to one single reason...
It's like falling in love–
they can't help it.

William Sherwood Fox

You can't say enough
about fishing.
Though the sport of kings,
it's just what the deadbeat ordered.

Thomas McGuane

There he stands,
draped in more equipment
than a telephone lineman,
trying to outwit an organism
with a brain no bigger than a breadcrumb,
and getting licked in the process.

Paul O'Neil

The literature of fly-fishing
is a minefield of disagreement
...on issues
of momentous inconsequence.

*Brian Clark
and John Goddard*

The aerospace industry
requires less technical jargon
than the average
bass fisherman.

Patrick F. McManus

On saltwater fishing:

Ahhh.
It is only for the strong man
with a hard stomach.
It is like sex
after lunch.

Charles Ritz

I will agree that worms
are not the ideal bait,
but if between worms
and an empty basket,
what will you?

O.W. Smith

[T]his planet
is covered with sordid men
who demand that he
who spends time fishing
shall show returns in fish.

Leonidas Hubbard, Jr.
(1902)

I fish better
with a lit cigar;
some people
fish better with talent.

Nick Lyons

I lost the second fly
and my cool right
about the same time.
"Quick!" I screamed.
"Give me another Bisexual!"

Judy Muller

Wading
The most common means
through which a dry-fly fisherman
is transformed into a wet-fly fisherman.

Henry Beard
and Roy Mckie

Trout...are perfectly content
with just more of the same,
as long as they live,
and
...are in no way concerned
with changing
or bettering their lot.

Arnold Gingrich

People who fish for food,
and sport be damned,
are called pot-fishermen.
The more expert ones are called
crack pot-fishermen.
All other fishermen are called
crackpot fishermen.
This is confusing.

Ed Zern

Most of us
will not wear out the knees
of our waders
while fly-fishing....
Cowboys or fly-casters,
we like to be tall in the saddle.

M.R. Montgomery

Only an extraordinary person
would purposely risk being outsmarted
by a creature
often less than twelve inches long,
over and over again.

Janna Bialek

[O]f all the liars
among mankind,
the fisherman
is the most trustworthy.

William Sherwood Fox

Nymph fishing
is comparable
to using a Ouija board.
You're never quite sure
if you're communicating with
the Other World
or not.

Jack Ohman

All the romance of trout fishing
exists in the mind of the angler
and is in no way shared by the fish.

Harold F. Blaisdell

[The end of my opening day
of trout season resembled]
a sardine can... assaulted with a cleaver.
A little ragged around the edges...
but indisputably opened.

Ben Hur Lampman

[T]wo fishermen
are a partnership,
while any more than that
constitutes a committee.

John Gierach

Herbert Hoover said
it was for fun, and to wash your soul,
and I don't say he was altogether wrong,
but I can't forget
that he was less than altogether right
about a number of things.

Arnold Gingrich

Many a beginner who cracks off his flies
pleases himself with the idea
that some trout of large dimensions
has carried them away.

W.C. Stewart
(1857)

All fishermen are liars;
it's an occupational disease with them
like housemaid's knee
or editor's ulcers.

Beatrice Cook

[C]atching fish
is as incidental to fishing
as making babies is
to _____.

William Humphrey

Fly equipment is so expensive
that many think
the Department of Defense
has it contracted out.

Jack Ohman

Contrary to common belief,
it is not true
that if you cut a worm-fisherman in half,
each half
will grow into a complete fisherman.
For which we should all be thankful.

Ed Zern

When a trout chooses to prey
upon what he thinks
is weaker than himself,
the angler ought not to be blamed for it.

George Washington Bethune
(1847)

Anglers...exaggerate grossly
and make gentle and inoffensive creatures
sound like wounded buffalo and
man-eating tigers.

Roderick Haig-Brown

There may be nothing on earth,
except perhaps an unsuccessful
bridge-club luncheon,
quite so boring as trolling.
Trol-l-l-l-ing.

Russell Chatham

[L]ike "military intelligence"
and "airline cuisine,"
"sopisticated angler" is an oxymoron.

Thomas McGuane

I am not against golf,
since I cannot but suspect
it keeps armies of the unworthy
from discovering
trout....

Paul O'Neil

President Hoover liked to fish.
He also needed a place
where he would not be bothered
by the little people
while he planned the Great Depression.

Howell Raines

Our fishing report
was brief and to the point:
slow in the mornings,
slow in the evenings,
and <u>real</u> <u>slow</u>
in the middle of the day.
Would you care for a beer?

John Gierach

There is,
among hard-core fishermen,
a conviction that the truth,
like pure water and the fish that live in it,
is a precious commodity,
not to be squandered or over-used.

Ed Zern

Fly-fishing is such great fun,
I have often felt,
that it really ought to be done
in bed.

Robert Traver

There is no greater fan
of fly fishing
than the worm.

Patrick F. McManus

Fishing has a reputation
as an innocuous,
fairly mindless pastime
enjoyed most by shiftless people.

Paul Schullery

Oh the gallant fisher's life!
It is the best of any;
'Tis full of pleasure, void of strife,
And tis beloved by many.

Izaak Walton
(1653)

The trout
do not rise in
[any] cemetery.

Sparse Grey Hackle

Knowing the Latin name
of the insect that is mysteriously absent
lets you piss and moan in a dead language,
but otherwise doesn't help much.

John Gierach

Two casts
from the bank
and I've got something:
a seventy-foot
pine tree.

Nick Lyons

The truth is,
fish have very little sex life.
If you have ever tried
to make love under water,
you will know why.

Ed Zern

A woman's place
is in her home water.
And for this woman,
that means water without men.
Or women.
Just me and the fish.

Judy Muller

If you've got short, stubby fingers
and wear reading glasses,
any relaxation
you would normally derive from fly fishing
is completely eliminated
when you try to tie on a fly.

Jack Ohman

The proper bait, live or artificial,
is what you took so much pains to
get yesterday
but which in your haste
to be off to-day
you left at home.

William Sherwood Fox

Salmon in Britain is poached...
in milk.
The taste is describable.
Poached Milk.

William Humphrey

Actually,
trout have little opportunity
to feed on earthworms,
other than those that are
draped on hooks.

Harold F. Blaisdell

The individual who owns
miles of stream
and invites no one to fish
is a monopolist
and should be dissolved
into his component parts
by the "Trout busters."

Arnold Gingrich

[F]ish are always two inches longer,
if not better than that,
before they are caught.
It is a very remarkable fact.

Ben Hur Lampman

Calling
fishing a hobby
is like calling
brain surgery
a job.

Paul Schullery

Fishermen
were not always so adept
at distance-casting...
they were great
skulkers and sneakers.

M.R. Montgomery

Fly fishermen spend hours
tying little clumps of fur
and feathers on hooks,
trying to make a trout fly
that looks a real fly.
But nobody has ever seen
a natural insect trying to mate
with a Fanwing Ginger Quill.

Ed Zern

The trout...
has more automatic controls
built into it
than a guided missile.
(They work a lot better, too.)

Sparse Grey Hackle

...as for Damming,
Groping, Spearing,
Hanging, Twitcheling,
Netting or Firing by night,
[I] esteem them
to be used only
by disorderly
and
rascally Fellows...

James Chetham
(1681)

If there is ever a revolution,
trout and salmon fishermen
will be the first to go up against the wall.
Black bass and bream fishermen
will either be in the audience or
the firing squad.

Russell Chatham

There are very few things in life
that are dead center.
Three of them are:
1955 Ford pickups, B.B. King,
and dry-fly fishing.

John Gierach

Fishing
is the most wonderful thing
I do in my life,
barring some equally
delightful unmentionables,
and not disregarding
gluttony and booze.
It's in the top five.

Jim Harrison

I once knew a guy
who spent five thousand dollars
traveling to Scotland
and staying at posh resorts.
He did not catch a fish.
I don't catch any on
West Eighty-Fourth Street, either.

Nick Lyons

Of all pursuits mankind has devised
to make you look stupid
and uncoordinated,
fly fishing
is unquestionably
number one.

Jack Ohman

I get all the truth I need
in the newspaper every morning,
and every chance I get I go fishing,
or swap stories with fishermen,
to get the taste of it
out of my mouth.

Ed Zern

[T]he fisherman
who isn't plagued
with suggestions
is fishing alone.

Beatrice Cook

I don't think there's any such thing
as one rod,
any more than there's such
a thing as one peanut.
Either you're eating peanuts
or you aren't.

Arnold Gingrich

In the world of fishing
there are magic phrases
that are guaranteed
to summon the demon.
Among them are: "remote trout lake,
"fish up to 13 pounds,"
"the place the guides fish
on their days off,"
and "my travel agent."

John Gierach

These brook trout
will strike any fly you present,
provided you don't get close enough
to present it.

Howell Raines
(quotes Dick Blalock)

In the future
I mean to be a fine
streamside entomologist.
I'm going to start on that
when I am much too old
to do any of the two thousand things
I can think of that are more fun
than screening insects
in cold running water.

Thomas McGuane

When I go fishing
I too want to get away from it all...
but I do not want to have
to go far to find it.

William Humphrey

The best way to learn
to be a fly fisherman
is to go to a river and ask the trout
for a few lessons.

Gwen Cooper
and Evelyn Haas

Since I began to fish
in the days before memory
and have no consciousness
of ever not fishing,
the evidence is clear
that I was born a fisherman.

Nick Lyons

I once heard a couple
of elderly bachelors...
arguing about whether
people spawned in the
spring or fall.
They asked several other
anglers to help settle the argument,
but nobody could remember.

Ed Zern

I visualize the system
[of calling bugs and things
by Latin names]
as a small pool of trout
surrounded
by a great wall of semantics.

Charles F. Waterman

Even eminent chartered accountants
are known, in their capacity as fishermen,
blissfully to ignore differences
between seven and ten inches,
half a pound and two pounds,
three fish and a dozen fish.

William Sherwood Fox

The leader settled
on the lowest branch of the bush
and the fly swung on its little pendulum
three or four inches from the water. . . .
It is the only time
I have ever fought a fish in a tree.

Norman Maclean

There will be days
when the fishing is better
than one's most optimistic forecast,
others when it is far worse.
Either is a gain
over just staying home.

Roderick Haig-Brown

Any time a man ain't fishin'
he's fritterin' away his life.

Patrick F. McManus

Nowhere in the Florida Fish and Game
regulations is anything said
about fly-fishing for gators,
probably for the same reason
that New Jersey has no open season
on elephants.

Red Smith

The only thing
I'm certain about today
is that what I don't know
about fishing would fill a book–
and it has.

Harold F. Blaisdell

When I cross over
the last current of all,
I confidently expect to see
a certain breed of sinners,
oblivious of their burns,
casting Rat-faced McDougalls
upon the waters
of the River Styx.

William Humphrey

Index to Source

(Quotations appear by page number)

19   Ray Bergman, *Trout* 2nd ed. (New York: Knopf, 1965) 257.

20   Arnold Gingrich, *The Fishing in Print: A Guided Tour Through Five Centuries of Fishing Literature* (New York: Winchester, 1974) 304.

21   Beatrice Cook, *Till Fish Do Us Part: The Confessions of a Fisherman's Wife* (New York: Morrow, 1949) 14.

22   William Humphrey, "Bill Breaks His Duck," *Open Season* (New York: Delacorte-Seymour Lawrence, 1986) 171-204.

23   Zern, *Hunting and Fishing* 36.*

24   Sparse Grey Hackle, *Fishless Days, Angling Nights* (New York: Crown, 1971) 167.

25   Haig-Brown, *River Never Sleeps* 268.*

26   Fox, *Silken Lines* 16-17.*

27   Thomas McGuane, *Silent Seasons*, ed. Russell Chatham (Livingston: Clark City Press, 1978) 1.

28   Paul O'Neil, "In Praise of Trout and Also Me,"*American Trout Fishing: Theodore Gordon and a Company of Anglers*, ed. Arnold Gingrich (New York: Knopf, 1965) 76.

29   Brian Clark and John Goddard, *The Trout and the Fly* (Norfolk: Page Bros., 1980) 130.

30   McManus, *Never Sniff a Gift Fish* 57.*

31   Charles Ritz, qtd in Nick Lyons, *Confessions of a Fly Fishing Addict* (New York: Fireside-Simon and Schuster, 1989) 50.

32   O. W. Smith, "The Shank of the Trout Season," *The Field and Stream Treasury of Trout Fishing* ed. Leonard M. Wright, Jr. (New York: Fawcett, 1986) 36-44.

33   Leonidas Hubbard, Jr., qtd in Raymond J. Pupedis "Don't Quote Me, But....," *Discovery* 23.2 (1992) 23-26. *

34   Nick Lyons, *Bright Rivers* (Philadelphia: Lippincott, 1977) 40.*

35   Judy Muller, "A Woman's Place," *Home Waters: A Fly-Fishing Anthology* ed.Gary Soucie (New York: Simon and Schuster, 1991) 96-100.

36   Henry Beard and Roy McKie, *fishing: An Angler's Dictionary* (New York: Workman, 1983) 88.

37   Gingrich, *Fishing in Print* 304.*

38   Ed Zern, *How to Tell Fish from Fishermen or a Plague on Both Your Houses* (New York: D. Appleton Century, 1947) 6.

39   Montgomery, *Way of the Trout* 226.*

40   Janna Bialek, "Thoughts from a Fishing Past," *Uncommon Waters: Women Write about Fishing*, ed. Holly Morris (Seattle: Seal Press, 1991) 161-168.

41   Fox, *Silken Lines* 115.*

42   Ohman, *Fear of Fly Fishing* 80.*

43   Harold F. Blaisdell, *The Philosophical Fisherman* (Boston: Houghton Mifflin, 1969) 53.

44   Ben Hur Lampman, *A Leaf from French Eddy: A Collection of Essays on Fish, Anglers and Fishermen* (Portland: Touchtone, 1965) 37.

45   Gierach, "Big Empty River," *View from Rat Lake* 7-24.*

46   Arnold Gingrich, qtd in Raymond J. Pupedis "Dont Quote Me, But....," *Discovery* 23.2 (1992) 23-26.

47   W. C. Stewart, *The Practical Angler* qtd in Gingrich, *The Fishing in Print* 143.*

48   Cook, *Till Fish Do Us Part*, 13.*

49   William Humphrey, "Cast and Cast Again," *Open Season* (New York: Delacorte-Seymour Lawrence, 1986) 99-126.

50   Ohman, *Fear of Fly Fishing* 11.*

51   Zern, *How to Tell Fish From Fishermen* 38.*

52   George Washington Bethune, introduction, *The Compleat Angler* qtd in Gingrich, *The Fishing in Print* 158.*

53   Roderick Haig-Brown, *Fisherman's Fall* (New York: Morrow, 1964) 86.

54   Russell Chatham, "Sterling Silver," *Silent Seasons* ed. Russell Chatham (Livingston: Clark City Press, 1978) 195-202.

55   Thomas McGuane, "Runoff," *Home Waters: A Fly-Fishing Anthology*, ed. Gary Soucie (New York: Simon and Schuster, 1991) 261-268.

56   O'Neil, "In Praise of Trout and Also Me," *American Trout Fishing* 71-72.*

57   Howell Raines, *Flyfishing Through the Mid-Life Crisis* (New York: Morrow, 1993) 18.

58   Gierach, *Sex, Death and Fly-fishing* 93.*

59   Zern, *Hunting and Fishing* 115.*

60   Traver, *Discovery* 25.*

61   McManus, *Never Sniff a Gift Fish* 157.*

62   Paul Schullery, "Home River," *Home Waters: A Fly-Fishing Anthology*, ed. Gary Soucie (New York: Simon and Schuster, 1991) 314-324.

63   Izaak Walton, *The Compleat Angler* (New York: The Worlds Classics-Oxford UP, 1982) 185.

64   Hackle, *Fishless Days* 167.*

65   Gierach, *Sex Death and Fly-fishing* 11.*

66   Lyons, *Bright Rivers* 45.*

67   Zern, *How to Tell Fish from Fishermen* 32.*

68   Muller, "A Woman's Place," *Home Waters* 96-100.*

69   Ohman, *Fear of Fly Fishing* 110.*

70   Fox, *Silken Lines* 19.*

71   William Humphrey, "The Spawning Run," *Open Season* (New York: Delacorte-Seymour Lawrence, 1986) 49-98.

72   Blaisdell, *Philosophical* 63.*

73 Arnold Gingrich, *American Trout Fishing: Theodore Gordon and a Company of Anglers*, ed. Arnold Gingrich (New York: Knopf, 1965) 15.

74 Lampman, *Leaf from French Eddy* 23.*

75 Schullery, "Home River," *Home Waters* 314-324.*

76 Montgomery, *Way of the Trout* 221.*

77 Zern, *Hunting and Fishing* 4.*

78 Hackle, *Fishless Days* 192-193.*

79 James Chetham, *Angler's Vade Mecum*, qtd in Gingrich, *The Fishing in Print* 65.

80 Russell Chatham, "Fishing: Mystiques and Mistakes," *Dark Waters* (Livingston: Clark City Press, 1988) 59-66.

81 Gierach, "The Purist," *View from Rat Lake* 53-69.*

82 Jim Harrison, *Silent Seasons* ed. Russell Chatham (Livingston: Clark City Press, 1978) 145.

83 Nick Lyons, "The Complete Book of Fly Fishing for Trout" *Confessions of a Fly Fishing Addict* (New York: Fireside-Simon and Schuster, 1989)133-136.

84 Ohman, *Fear of Fly Fishing* 11.*

85 Zern, *Hunting and Fishing* 115.*

86 Cook, *Till Fish Do Us Part* 145.*

87 Gingrich, *Fishing in Print* 329.*

88 Gierach, introduction, *View from Rat Lake* 1.*

89 Raines, *Flyfishing Through the Mid-Life Crisis* 18.*

90 Thomas McGuane, *An Outside Chance: Essays on Sport* (New York: Penguin, 1982) 164.

91 Humphrey, "My Moby Dick," *Open Season* 1-48.*

92 Cooper, Haas, *Wade a Little Deeper* 36.*

93 Nick Lyons, "First Trout, First Lie," *The Field and Stream Treasury of Trout Fishing*, ed. Leonard M. Wright, Jr. (New York: Fawcett-Columbine, 1986) 236-243.

94 Zern, *How to Tell Fish From Fishermen* 42.*

95 Charles F. Waterman, "Reel Cliques and Stiff Leaders" *Silent Seasons*, ed. Russell Chatham (Livingston: Clark City Press, 1978) 137-143.

96 Fox, *Silken Lines* 117.*

97 Norman Maclean, *A River Runs Through It* (Chicago: U of Chicago P, 1976) 43.

98 Roderick Haig-Brown, *Fisherman's Spring* (Toronto: Collins, 1951) 100.

99 McManus, *Never Sniff a Gift Fish* 25.*

100 Red Smith, "Everglades," *The Fly Fisher's Reader*, ed. Leonard M. Wright, Jr. (New York: Fireside-Simon and Schuster, 1990) 190-194.

101 Blaisdell, introduction *Philosophical* vi.*

102 Humphrey, "My Moby Dick" *Open Season* 8.*

        * See earlier listing for complete bibliographic entry.